DO YOU WANT A BOZO OR A BOAZ?

By
SHIRLEY A. MYERS

© 2020 by Shirley A. Myers

Do you Want a Bozo or a Boaz?

Printed in the United States of America

ISBN: 978-0-578-74131-4

All Scripture references are taken from the KING JAMES VERSION (KJV): KING JAMES VERSION, public domain.

Editor: Armor of Hope Writing & Publishing Services

∞ACKNOWLEDGEMENTS∞

This book could not, would not, have been written without the unction of the Holy Spirit. I am eternally grateful for the Holy Spirit's leading, for His guidance and teaching.

I also must thank my family- particularly my husband, Gordon and my oldest daughter, Dan-Yel, who supported me in this endeavor.

Two sisters in the ministry, Cynthia Parchman and Janice Robinson encouraged me and told me, "You've got to get this book done because people need it."

Last, but by no means least, I would like to thank my pastor, Apostle Julius H. Kidd, who from the moment I told him the title of the book said, "Catchy Title. I like it!" His support was crucial.

May God bless you all as He continues to use us in His great ministry.

CONTENTS

PREFACE
DO YOU WANT A BOZO OR A BOAZ?

So, what do you want in a husband? *Why do you want to be married?*

These are questions I have asked many young (and older) women. A real defining moment comes when I've asked: Do you want to get married, or do you want to be married? You see, many women spend more time getting ready for the wedding than they do preparing to be married.

These are questions women have to ask themselves, and while they are pondering, they must be brutally honest with themselves, listening for what comes from their hearts. Sometimes this isn't easy, but it is a necessary prerequisite to spending a lot of dough on a marriage that may or may not last past the honeymoon.

This book came about as a result of what started as a "basement" Bible study held in my home. It was a Bible study strictly for women. I held the study from 2004 to 2009.

As I conducted these studies, the Lord spoke to me about the Book of Ruth, specifically about how Ruth came to be Boaz's wife. The Lord wanted me to compare the character of Boaz, a wealthy landowner, to the character of a "Bozo," a clown or buffoonish-type character—one who is not serious about his treatment of women. Oh! He's lovable and funny, but he's not in relationships for the long haul.

The Holy Spirit gave me two monikers: one for Bozo— "Brothers on Zero," often juxtaposed with one for Boaz— "Brothers Orbiting around Zenith." From there, the ministry took off! The women were excited, engaged, energized and empowered!

I felt I was on the right track to teach women from the Word of God and what to look for in a husband. Conversely, we sought to teach them who to stay away from, or the "Bozos" of this world.

I've found that many, many young women want happily ever after, but they fail to realize the fairy tale's just that, a fairy tale, told and retold, but one that's not exactly true.

My prayer while working on and writing this book is that each woman who reads it will find strength to be satisfied in her "singleness" until her Boaz comes.

It's so appealing when women serve the Lord while single. Our singleness might just be the appetizer for the fabulous carmel, café au'lait, or chocolate desert, that's on the way. Imagine that!

I thank God for this precious jewel of a ministry, and for the women who will benefit from it.

Enjoy being satisfied and single while serving the Lord, as you await the arrival of your Boaz!

To God be the glory and all the honor forever and ever! Amen!

Now, let's take a journey back to the times of the judges. Let's see what blessings God has prepared for women everywhere. Walk with me into the eighth book of the Old Testament, the book of Ruth. Ready? Set? Go!

CHAPTER 1
-MAKING GOOD CHOICES-

"But one thing is needed, and Mary has chosen that good part, which will not be taken away from her." (Luke 10:42).

In Ruth chapter 1, Naomi tells the girls: "Look, girls, I'm going back to my homeland. My husband's dead, my sons are dead. There is really no reason to stay on in Moab. You girls must decide what you're going to do. I cannot make this decision for you." She tells them further to "return to your family." She uses the words turn and return over and over. "Return" is used six times in chapter one.

Then comes Orpah's decision in verse 14 of chapter 1. Orpah cries and she kisses her mother-in-law and says a fond farewell. On the other hand, Ruth's decision is quite dramatic – poetic even. Her decision will ring for all eternity throughout the annals of biblical history: "Don't ask me to leave you or stop following you. Where you go, I'll go. Your people will be my people. Your God, my God." It seems Ruth chose that "good part," the part mentioned in Luke 10:42: One thing (a meal) would have been enough, but Martha went to extremes to impress Jesus, thus causing her own dilemma! Mary chose what was better for her—worshipping at Jesus' feet! Ruth wanted the better, Orpah settled. (Isn't that the way it is for many women dating or looking for husbands today? Many settle for less than God's best, causing their own dilemmas!) Notice also, Ruth chose Naomi's God. Furthermore, the Bible tells us Ruth was "steadfastly-minded" to go to Bethlehem. She was absolutely determined to go with her mother-in-law. Orpah not so much. Ruth's mind was made up! She wanted to pursue God. She chose Him over Molech and Moab's other gods. She wanted something better.

Perhaps Ruth had heard Naomi talk about her God. We can't know for sure, but somehow Ruth made a firm decision. Look at Ruth's resolve to follow Naomi and to follow her God! You, too, must choose wisely. To forsake all and follow God. Life's all about choices.

We tell children in school: You must make good choices. Ruth made a decision to leave Moab and to follow Naomi's God. She was determined.

I've used a moniker, HALT, that I learned a long time ago. I don't remember from where, but I want you to learn it, too, as you make choices in your life. We'll talk about that later.

In chapter 4 of Matthew, we see the Temptation of Christ. Jesus has just left the Jordan River after having been baptized. He's been fasting and praying. He's <u>full</u> of the Holy Ghost. He is led into the wilderness to be tempted by Satan for forty days and forty nights.

It is on this scripture that the moniker HALT hangs. These accounts are mentioned in both Luke and Matthew. Satan tempts our Lord in three areas: physical appetite, worldly ambition, and spiritual attainment. Remember, the first man, Adam, failed where Jesus triumphed over Satan once and for all.

To continue, the Bible says in Luke 4:22 that Jesus had not been eating because He was fasting. When the fasting was over, He was hungry. It was then that the tempter came! "If thou be the Son of God, command these stones that it be made bread."

Notice with every temptation, Jesus counters with the Word of Almighty God! "It is written that man shall not live by bread alone, but by every word that proceedeth out of the mouth of God." (Matthew 4:4) And the text goes on with our Lord and Savior, Jesus Christ slaying Satan with the Word. Satan wanted Jesus to choose unwisely.

So, we use the moniker HALT because the enemy will come when you're **"H"** – hungry-physically or spiritually. (In the case of our text, Jesus was, in fact, (physically) hungry. Also, the enemy comes when you're **"A"**– angry. I allowed Satan to use me for years because I had an angry temper. I realized as an adult, this was because I had been molested as a child. So, I remind you how dangerous an angry temper can be. It can certainly keep you from making good choices.

In Genesis, Cain killed his brother Abel in part because he had a very bad temper. God cautioned Cain about his choices. Later, we find Cain not only murdered Abel, but buried him in a shallow grave. But Abel's blood "cried out" to God from the ground. Be very, very careful with anger. The Bible tells us, "Be ye angry, but sin not." (Ephesians 4:26)

Another way the enemy gains control over us is **"L"** – loneliness. I've taught the Word where I've asked women: "Have you ever been lonely in a crowded room?" Music's playing, people are laughing and talking, but you're lonely. The answer always comes back as yes.

We know that being alone is not always a lonely place. You can be alone but not lonely. Loneliness can cause us to settle for Mr. Right Now, rather than wait for God's very best. Proclaim God as Ruth did: "Your God shall be my God" (Ruth 1:16). Make Him your first choice! You can date yourself or get to know yourself while waiting on the Lord to choose our husband. With Him, you're never alone!

The last part of HALT deals with the letter T. The "**T**" stands

for "tired." When you're tired spiritually or physically, Satan will take advantage of this condition. He will whisper things, make suggestions to you, hoping you will bite. He will try to get you to do what you otherwise wouldn't when you're rested, or when you've been in the Word and **doing it.**

So HALT!

Why? Because making the wrong choices may mean incalculable losses which will echo for posterity.

So again... HALT!

CHAPTER 2
-WHAT'S IN A NAME?

"Call me Marah: for the Lord has dealt very harshly with me..." (Ruth 1:20).

Naomi says in the Book of Ruth chapter 1 that she sees herself as "**Marah**" rather than "pleasant." Why? Well, she answers us in Ruth 1:20: "And she said unto them (the women who inquired), "Call me not Naomi. Call me Marah, for the Lord has dealt very bitterly with me." Don't call me by my real name, Naomi or "pleasant. Call me "Marah," for I'm a bitter woman.

Because of so much loss, Naomi's personality, the way she saw the world, and possibly her outlook on life, went from a pleasant point of view to a bitter outlook. This is not unusual when one suffers so much loss. It's not just normal for the one who has experienced such loss to be bitter. It's also not unusual for others' personalities, and the way they relate to us, to change. This also occurs when we gain some things, i.e., get a diploma, get married, buy a new car or house. I suppose the key is <u>not</u> to let things—sad or otherwise—change us, except for the better.

Naomi says in verse 21 of chapter 1, "I went out full, and the Lord has brought me home again empty…" She had a husband and two sons, and I presume a decent life when she left Bethlehem to move to Moab. Possibly she had a decent life in Moab for a while, but she tells the curious inquiring women that she has returned to Bethlehem empty and bitter.

Empty and bitter! You've heard or perhaps you've said about someone yourself: She's just bitter and empty. We as women say those things about each other, don't we? Sadly, yes we do!

Ladies, don't let bitterness become your ring bearer. I've always said, "You can choose to become better, rather than bear the burden of bitterness." You are not what happened to you! Amen? Amen!

You may need to, at long last, confront your affinity and fondness for these scrub-like characters you've allowed to waste your time. Ask yourself: "Is there some deficit in me that attracts these losers?" Figure out what's really eating you when you choose men with dubious names and/or reputations, because it eats you up. Is this peccadillo why you attract Bozos? It's not by happenstance.

Choose to see what you see. "Eyes wide open." Be bold. There are too many instances when I speak to women that I just know that they know these guys are not of good character/reputation. Oh yes, you know it! The light bulb—no, the marquee—is flashing over their heads: "Oh say can you see!"

You have perhaps heard of the man's reputation and seen his reckless actions. Yet, you're still drawn to him, fully intrigued, interested. Remember this behavior speaks volumes about him.

Ruth and Orpah may have been with sickly, weak, failing men, but perhaps they (the men) presented themselves well. This is common, isn't it? In this day and age, you too may be with such men. Men who "present themselves well," but maybe are wolves in sheep's clothing. Look deep before you leap!

Look at the name. Closely inspect it. Be alert to how the men "wear" their names. Listen to what others say about them.

Oh! I know you don't believe 'em, but are many people saying the same thing? What is his behavior when you're at the barbeque? At family gatherings? What about football games? What happens when his team is losing? Does he utter a barrage of epitaphs? Does he turn into a cussing cistern after a few drinks? How is he in gridlock traffic? What makes him angry? How does he behave when the job he had dried up? He will eventually <u>show</u> you who he really, really is. Remember: Don't be afraid to "see what you see." Of course, once you see it, you must deal with it! You have to do something about your situation.

If the dude's a Bozo, you are going to know it. Maya Angelou had it right: "When someone shows you who they are, believe them." But sadly, we want these Bozos to be the ideal we've had in our heads for so long, the one we created.

I'm sure Nabal's wife, Abigail over in 1 Samuel, chapter 25, verses 1 to 38, really wanted Nabal to be a prince, but the Bible tells us Nabal was a <u>fool</u>. Nabal was so much a fool that Abigail had to step in and speak with King David to spare Nabal's life. How much are you willing to risk? How long have you been throwing this (drowning) man a life-line? Well, here's a news flash: Let somebody else save him!

You're not his therapist, nurse-maid, or mother. And, you certainly should not marry him!

Character—integrity, humility, kindness, patience—all must be hallmarks of a man of good standing. Check again, or rather shake that apple tree to see if apples fall out. If coconuts fall out of his apple tree, you've got a problem.

CHAPTER 3
-MOVING OUTTA MOAB-
(MOAB: "Moving On After Bozo")

"Wherefore she went out of the place (Moab) where she was..." (Ruth 1:7).

Let's briefly discuss our reference to Moab, the country of Ruth and her sister-in-law, Orpah. Here I use the moniker MOAB: Moving On After Bozo. As the Bible states in the Book of Ruth chapter 1, verse 1, Elimelech and his wife Naomi initially left Bethlehem Judah to go to Moab because there was a famine in their own country. Moab was an agriculturally successful country, thus the couple's move to do better.

While in Moab, their sons Chilion and Mahlon marry Moabitess women, Ruth and Orpah. At some point all these men die, leaving behind three widows. While we don't know just how long the family lived in Moab, we do know and understand from scripture that the men died. To be a widow in these times was a difficult plight. We cannot say for certain how much more difficult the lives of these three women became <u>before </u>Naomi decided to return to Bethlehem Judah. What we do know from scripture is that Naomi made a wise decision, one that was providential, divine even. Interestingly, she implored her daughters-in-law to stay on in Moab. Orpah decided, "You're right, Mom. I'll stay on in my country." But according to scripture and our narrative in the Book of Ruth, specifically verses 16-18 of chapter 1, daughter-in-law Ruth was determined to go on to Bethlehem Judah with her mother-in-law Naomi. Somehow this reminds me of the story of Martha and Mary in the New Testament. Martha's very busy preparing for a visit with Jesus. Once He arrives, Martha implores Jesus to get Mary to help her prepare meals. Mary had been sitting at the feet of

Jesus, worshipping. Apparently, Martha is so very flustered. Jesus tells her (in a nice way): "Martha! Martha! You're concerned about too many things." He says further: "Mary's chosen that good part which will not be taken away from her." (Luke 10:41-42)

Here in scripture, Ruth did what Mary did. She chose the good part. She made an informed decision to leave Moab. The past was over. The future was ahead of her.

New Testament scripture tells us in the Book of Philippians 3:14, "Putting those things which are behind me, and straining forward to what lies ahead, I press toward the mark for the prize of the high calling which is in Christ Jesus." Sometimes God has just moved on, and so should we.

So why did Ruth leave? We can't possibly know how she came to such an informed decision. Perhaps it was as simple as she didn't want her mother-in-law traveling alone. What we know for absolute certain is that Ruth was determined from her core to leave Moab. Her mind was completely made up!

When you want out of a situation or circumstance, you must have a made-up mind. I believe, and we should all concur, based on what we read in our narrative in Ruth chapter 1, Ruth knew exactly what she wanted and why. Of course, the decision to stay on in Moab, made by Orpah, is less clear.

While Orpah's choice is less clear, we could surmise she wasn't willing to leave hearth and home and all that Moab meant to her. Moab symbolizes here for Orpah, familiarity and comfort – what she knew. That's Moab. For our purposes here, I ask you, what is the definition of insanity? It is doing the same thing over and over and expecting a different result. Moab, by virtue of its familiarity and sinful comfort, is total insanity.

I've known women whose living arrangements weren't ideal and in some cases were petty dire. In some of these cases, their significant others, i.e., boyfriends, husbands, etc., were alcoholics, drug users, batterers, or all of the above. Yet, the women knew who they were and knew what to expect from them—a few smacks upside their heads, yes, but by nightfall, the "honeymoon" phase would start. Stay out all night drunk, yes, but they will come back home. Familiarity.

One thing you must have, you gotta have, is determination. Yes, determination like Ruth. You must have a made-up mind to have something better.

The path forward will be the unknown. The unknown can be fraught with many questions, twists and turns, and uncertainty. But if you take a step, the Lord will take you the rest of the way. When your situation's on zero, you can at least look up. Once you look up, you must get up and get out!

Please remember your indecision could allow you to miss out on the very best blessings the Lord has for you. In getting out of Moab, "pray and weigh," then get away! Prayerfully consider what you need to do. God moves miraculously through prayer. Make it a priority. And, be specific. Tell God what you want and what you need. <u>Write it down</u>. See it in black and white and red as you plead the blood of Jesus over your requests. Then, "walk it out."

Let us revisit he story of Blind Bartimaeus where Jesus asks the blind man: "What do you want me to do for you?"

(Mark 10:51)

Bartimaeus is very specific. He also is quite determined to make himself heard. He shouts and he shouts, and he shouts, "That I may recover my sight." So, we see Bartimaeus receiving what he desired most: to see.

You, like Bartimaeus, want to see. You want to see what else the Lord has for you. Inwardly you know *there's got to be more than this for me!* You're correct. There is!

If perhaps your getting out of Moab is a dangerous proposition. Save some money, pack a survival bag, and tell one very trusted person of what your plans are. You may even have to consult law enforcement, because your mess in Moab may be more than you can handle alone. Get God involved, and get Him involved quickly, without delay.

The Bozo you're currently with has shown his true colors once too often. You've seen his bombastic, abusive, bellicose behavior for months or perhaps for years.

You wanted to fix him, help him, and mother him. He wanted to wreck you and you helped him do it. Yes! You were complicit in this Moab mess. Admit it! He's been reared. You're not his mother, not his priest. Stop attracting men who need managing, swaddling, babying. If this is what is going on now, imagine marrying such a man! Who did you turn down? Keep your plans secret, because moving out is a dish best served cold!

You will have a palpable sense of apprehension, but you are not alone. Your desire to remove yourself from a sinking ship is a testament to your inner strength. The Lord is at hand. Be brave, bold, and completely assured that better is on the horizon. His name's Boaz!

Can't you see this dude isn't about to change! He's not who you've tried to make him out to be. He's not some Hollywood bad boy needing rescue, cneeding love from the right woman to turn him around. Your silence in this terribly sad soap opera makes you complicit in this scenario.

Sometimes when you're trying to get out of Moab, you need what Naomi had. She had a "goel," a Kinsman redeemer. Boaz was such a man, a goel, or Kinsman redeemer. In essence, he was a type of Christ. In the Book of Ruth chapter 2 and verse 1, Boaz is called by the name "Kinsman of her husband." He's portrayed as a mighty man of wealth, one of Elimelech's relatives.

Who you may need to get out of your personal Moab is someone like a pastor, a teacher, or a trusted relative, someone whose heart is bent towards you, a person of compassion and caring. You need a praying soul, a person of integrity who will help you get your proverbial act together. Also, alas, you need to help yourself!

I want you to watch this: In the Book of Ruth, chapter 2, verse 2, it was Ruth herself who when she was told about Boaz, suggested to Naomi that she should go to the field "to work." What? Ruth wanted to get a job! Yes, so you make sure you have funds or the wherewithal to "fund" your escape from Moab. Save some money for those crazy, scary, rainy days. Moab can have days of dilemmas. What else could you do? Why you could finish your education. Work on you!

If children are involved, think about their well-being in this mess called Moab. Are they safe? Think about how they feel. They deserve the very best you that you can be. Don't let the messaging they receive in Moab be,

"Sorry child/children, this is all you deserve!" Don't subject them to an endless eddy of meandering men who won't commit. Think of how they feel seeing one Bozo after another come through like a turnstile. Abusive men. Cussing men. Volatile men. Drunkards. Drug abusers.

"No man is in so much peril as he/she who can't see danger." When you know you've been in a dark place for a long time, and when you know your situation is going nowhere fast, you need to move outta Moab!

While Ruth was on the road to Bethlehem-Judah, she had no clue she was actually on the pathway to promise, provision, and prosperity. This fact from this Old Testament narrative should be a big enough incentive to leave your own Moab. Timing is everything.

I can just imagine Ruth in the mirror on her wedding day: "I'm actually marrying Boaz! OMG! I got outta Moab!" Out of loss, pain and paganism came blessing and betrothal. Oh ladies, you can't imagine what <u>God</u> has prepared for you! Scripture tells us, "Eyes haven't seen, nor have ears heard nor has it entered into the heart of man, what God has prepared for those who love Him" (1 Corinthians 2:9).

Listen: The funeral dirges Ruth had heard replayed in her head when Elimelech, Chilion, and Mahlon died may have created some discouragement, some desperate dawns, some "I laid awake at night" moments for Ruth. Perhaps she had a lot on her plate when she left Moab and her family members, but she stepped out of misery on the wings of sheer faith and determination. She believed to see God's goodness in a new land. Way to go, Ruth!

Moab had become too small to hold her dreams and aspirations. Mess was in Moab. Missteps were in Moab. Mistakes and misery were in Moab. Yet up ahead of her was a miracle!

Oh, I'm here to tell you, you can get out! HOW BADLY DO YOU WANT IT? You have to really, really want it. Faith involves taking action. One can imagine Ruth's anxiety, her trepidation at leaving her homeland and her family's way of life. Leaving the pagan way of life for Bethlehem—leaving pagan worship that was so comfortable—this was a huge move. Loss will cause you to either move or stand as a deer caught in headlights. Loss led her to move out. Fresh start. New venue. New life. New love.

My mind's eye conjures up images of Ruth's travel to Bethlehem-Judah – feet tired, calloused, dirty and swollen. Perhaps she shed salty tears intermittently mixed with the prospect of what her future held. Through it all, Ruth pressed her way, on and on and on.

So now you see you, too, must press. You must move. Move. Press. Move. Press. As you go, remember all things are under God's purview and He knows the plans He has for you (Jeremiah 29:11): "I know the thoughts I have concerning you...to give you an expected end (a future), hope..." Something that would manifest for you.

God's word is a sure word, ladies! So what do you say? Well, I say, "Get to steppin'!"

S – t – e – p!

A Short Story

May I tell you something of a short story here?

One evening I was teaching "Do you want a Bozo or a Boaz?" from my home. There were quite a few young (and older) women in my basement that evening. Prior to this evening, the Lord gave me a specific vignette to tell the women. He wanted me to call the vignette "A Rainy Night in Georgia." It went thusly:

"You'd been trying to get out of this relationship, but the sex was so good, you can't imagine life without it, or without the man. But now you've come to a place where you really know that you must end this yo-yo of a relationship. Tonight, it's raining, as you ponder your decision. Suddenly, the doorbell rings, startling you. You peek out your window. OMG! It's him! Why is he here in this terrible weather? Why can't he just leave you alone! You struggle to know <u>what</u> to do. He knows you are at home. He's seen your car. What to do! He rings your doorbell incessantly. Finally, you decide to answer, asking, "who's there?" The answer comes back: "Come on, _____. Open the door, Girl! It's raining hard out here. Come on, please!" Against your better judgement, you crack the door. "Go home! I'm not letting you in. Leave me alone! Why are you here?"

He pleads and pleads and so you relent. There he is, standing in your living room, soaking wet, the light causing his skin to glisten. He pulls a Billy Dee Williams (for you youngsters, watch <u>Lady Sings the Blues</u> with Diana Ross and Billy Dee Williams). "Hey, are you gonna just let me stand here soaking wet? Get me a towel, please." He asks you to help dry him off. It's now that you remember what you've tried so hard to forget! So now here you are - the two of you on the floor.

Ladies, at this point during the teaching, the silence is broken as a young woman screams out, "OMG! That's what happened to me!" At this point, everybody's stunned.

At the end of the teaching, this young woman stayed behind while the other women left. She told me that this rainy night's dalliance left her pregnant!

This young woman was not only mired in Moab, she was now stuck, because there was going to be another life to take care of. Sadly, the young man left her to go on with his life, leaving the young woman holding the proverbial bag.

I've often said to young women, "When he (Bozo) falls asleep in your bed after lovemaking, while he's snoring and snoozing on your 1,000 count sheets and down comforter, look at him from head to toe and ponder this: What if I get pregnant? Would this man be there for me? From his hairline to his heels, ponder this. Then remind yourself that you were not protected or taken care of when he gave you several STDs. He was not there when you had to see an abortionist alone. You'll never get better if you don't require more!

In the world we live in today, sadly, Moab's still alive and well. Moab's a real place, but you don't have to set up a permanent residence there. You can move.

You gotta' get out! You gotta' get out and you gotta' stay out! Make that move and make it now!

CHAPTER 4
-DEAD THINGS-

"And Elimelech, Naomi's husband died; and she was left, and her two sons, Mahlon and Chilion died also..." (Ruth 1:3,5).

We find that Naomi, Ruth and Orpah are all widows, their husbands deceased. They are women alone in a world where it was dangerous for women to be alone. These women have buried husbands, with no idea of what would come next. Theirs was a fairly serious predicament.

So, what does come next, after a bad break-up? After the death of a relationship? My own suggestion would be for you to do an "autopsy" on every "dead" relationship. This will allow you to figure out if some part of your "stuff", i.e., your lack of vision, your personality, and your negativity for example contributed to your relationship dying. What contributed to its demise? Can you see a pattern in each one?

I've often thought of some of Hollywood's most talented, most beautiful actresses/actors, and I've been heard to say, "They keep choosing the wrong man/woman. They seem more interested in choosing Mr. /Ms. Right Now over Mr. /Ms. Right. The only common denominator is him/her."

So, do an in-depth and thorough autopsy. Search your spiritual heart's chambers. See if you are complicit in the demise of these damnable alliances.

Could it be possible that you are unwittingly choosing the same kind of man? This present one is six-foot-four, blacker than the blackest blackberry, fine, educated, has a nice job, sweet personality. The next one's a cup of café' au lait, five-foot-eight with nice soft, brown eyes that twinkle. He caters to your every need but explodes at the mere mention of an old lover's name. (Any of this sound familiar?)

Be assured, Ruth, you must let go of dead things, of stinky, stagnant relationships. Yesterday's past and gone. Your future is up ahead. Live in the here and now. Heal old hurts. Mourn, but don't allow mourning to become the clothes you wear daily. Get down to what's ailing you! Putting Band-Aids on gaping wounds will only temporarily take care of the matter, and you know this!

Here's another nugget. Ladies, stop behaving as if you can't recognize a dead thing, a Bozo, when you see him. The truth of the matter is, sometimes you do! First impression, second, right down to a year or more later. You may have wasted your time, energy and Love on a Loser. Remember: If it ain't going up, it's coming down. If it ain't marriage, it just may be a mishap, a mistake. Bury all those deceased things. Some of those relationships, if you're honest, were DOA. Do that autopsy! These relationships are not sustainable.

Get rid of riff-raff. Position yourself to be blessed with your Boaz. Kiss Kevin goodbye. Say Adios to Adam. Arrivederci to Aaron. Haven't you hooked your wagon to a horseless carriage? Surely as these types of relationships go on, you can see what the end will be. Use an abundance of caution dealing with Bozos.

You are worthy of real love. You're attractive, intelligent, vibrant and vivacious. Sadly, because you've become accustomed to and entangled with mess and with so much drama for so long, you begin to question your own intuition, your own sense of what is good for you. Your own sense of who you are.

The messages on social media, the internet, and from your friends all tell you that you must behave a certain way. You must weigh a certain amount. (Note: My girls were taught, "You are more than the sum of your anatomical parts.") Like diamonds, we women are multifaceted, brilliant and beautiful.

You will, after break-ups, be bombarded with books and seminars of "this is what you ought to do" statements in the guise of advice. How do you meander through the mind-blowing, minefields of minutia you're receiving? Most importantly, remember: You belong to the Lord. You're vivacious, yes! You're intelligent, yes! But you're also a child of the Kingdom, and as such, you're vital to it and to God. You belong to the Lord!

The Bible declares in 1 Peter 3:3-4, "We are not to let our adornment be just outward adorning, but let it be the hidden man of the heart, a meek and quiet spirit, which is in the sight of God, of great price." You matter to the Lord!

As you do your autopsies, ask yourself: Do I see myself as attracting the wrong men? Then ask yourself why. Peel the layers of that onion back, Ruth. How do you feel about yourself right now? Do you see yourself as whole only when you're attached to someone else? If so, delve deep into the reason for that. There are reasons—sometimes good ones—for why some of your reckless relationships die a slow, agonizing death. Perhaps you're conflict avoidant and fearful. Delve deep to find out what is really going on. Face unpleasant truths head on! Then, vow to resolve the issues.

I'm reminded of the time one of my daughters was dating a fine young man—one with a good job, a very nice car, a great education and a beautiful apartment. My inner man was quite unsettled concerning this young man at a certain point. Over time, I felt led to ask her some more questions about him: Has he ever shown jealousy towards you having other male friends? Her answer shocked me as well as disturbed me. Also, it disturbed me concerning a comment he made in my home one Sunday after a worship service he attended. (He wasn't saved at the time). These things, plus the unsettled feelings I'd had about this young man's background caused me great concern. I began to pray mightily concerning the person my daughter thought she would marry. They had returned from a trip abroad, and my husband was quite excited, because he told me, "I feel he'll give her a ring soon. Maybe on this trip." I knew I had to pray fervently for an answer to my prayer: "Lord, is he the one for my daughter? Lord, if not, please show me! And show me he did! On a Sunday morning after another church service, the

Lord spoke, and he showed me the husband she is presently married to. But before that, she went through some on and off again relationships with this young man. Finally, after I prayed what I call the Boaz Prayer, this young man was finally gone for good! It was a difficult time for us all.

Sometimes, ladies, we must come to a place where we fully realize, albeit sadly, that "this" relationship is over! It's a very tough reality to grapple with agonizing, heart-breaking and possibly traumatic yet, we must get there. We must go through—and go through we shall—but if, as we say, "God brings us to it, He will take us through it." It really is for our good.

We just can't imagine <u>what</u> and sometimes <u>who</u> the Lord is keeping us from and why.

Now, I must tell you: The former young man went on to marry someone else. He just wasn't who God had for my daughter. You see, I firmly believe the Lord intervened. He knew what was up ahead, although everything (especially to my husband), looked fine. Once I asked her some questions, I saw clearly what the Lord was telling me! And, as difficult as it was, I knew this relationship would not last, and that this latest break-up would be their last. It was over! You see, the Lord sees all. He sees the end from the beginning. He sees behind every heart. Everything is under His purview! He knows what is best.

He intervenes in the affairs of mankind with love and compassion to accomplish his own divine will. And, if you're perfectly honest, there are some days you shout, "Thank you, Lord!" Because he spared you heartache and heartbreak beyond measure with some of these Bozos you've dated. Amen, somebody!

I must share with you that my daughter's been married now 14 years to a wonderful young man.

One famous ballplayer said, "It ain't over till it's over." I guess you have to be smart enough to recognize "over."

The dead things, i.e., dead relationships of your past should be buried and not revisited if they were caustic, toxic, traumatic or tenuous. It's over now. Move on! Have that funeral for all those ol' dead relationships and bury them all. You should realize God has promised you His best! Isn't that good news?

CHAPTER 5
-WASH-

"Wash thyself therefore, and anoint thee, and put thy raiment upon thee..." (Ruth 3:3).

If you're to be a Ruth, you have to wash! "Go wash!" Naomi tells Ruth. Perfume your body. Make your appearance presentable. Wash away the stench of Moab—the dusty, dirty, disgusting memories of Moab and all that occurred there. Move faithfully forward. Wash away the pain and negativity. The hurt. All that drama! Yes, you may have caused some hurts yourself. Wash it all away!

Moab felt normal because you'd been in it for so long. But it wasn't normal. You may have to be alone for a minute. Date yourself. It isn't so bad. Nor is knowing who and whose you are—now that's another story. Purposely and intentionally be alone. Put all those rocks you've been rolling away. Remember you're not alone: The Lord is with you always.

Go wash! Wash away all that is past tense. Get yourself up and get going. You went to the nail shop alone. You grocery shopped alone, went to the spa alone—before Ricky, before Billy and Willie and Jamar. Do this for yourself. Aren't you worth it?

Take all that maudlin memorabilia—the pictures, letters, texts from old lovers, and place them in file thirteen. Lose those lemons. Kick those keepsake boxes of confusion to the curb. Clean out your closet of any and all reminders of these worthless worms. Call Goodwill. That's what they're for! "U-haul" butt!

Moab's over! Bethlehem's ahead of you. Stop curling up with the Lifetime channel of what could've been. You must remember: Bozo is counting on you to be emotional, to keep your emotions raw, make you vulnerable. This may cause you to roll that "old" rock of a <u>wreck</u> right back into your new reality. He can't come back. Don't let him!

Stop memorializing his good attributes. These old memories are just the type of things that leave you prey for predatory men with plenty of bad intentions and no direction or integrity.

What you need to do after Moab is just breathe for now. B–r–e–a–t–h–e. Inhale. Exhale. Take stock of where you are and believe whose you are. You belong to the Lord! You were His <u>first</u>.

Always bear in mind: Rico wrecked your life. Billy was just plain silly. You must wash. Clean house - ridding yourself of these ridiculous reality show-type men. Clean. Throw away. Give away everything related to that "rock" lest you go overboard and drown with that proverbial rock wrapped around your pretty little neck like an albatross.

Wash! Bathe! Make room for what and who God has for you. Pretty Pooky's out, and Boaz is on your horizon. Make room, Ruth. Wash! You surely don't want the decomp of those old dead relationships to cause you to miss out on God's best! The decomp of weak, sickly or dead relationships will surely repel potential Boazes.

Usually women who've been hurt badly by Bozos will "nurse and rehearse" the times they were wounded. Thus, with every new relationship, the baggage they carry multiplies. Imagine the load as you bear it. Every man who hurt you is in that baggage. Six-foot-four is in there! Five-foot-eight is in there! Caramel complexion's there! Café au latte is in there! That luggage is quite a lot to lug around, isn't it? Don't do it anymore. Wash! Remove every trace of these tragic, <u>trifling</u> relationships.

-<u>In The Field</u>-

I find it remarkable and reassuring that Ruth ends up by chance in the field of Boaz. Of course, we fully and firmly realize that this was no accident! Rather, it was the providence of Almighty God. This was His plan all along. God doesn't make mistakes or do things haphazardly. Ruth starts her fantastic journey into the lineage of Jesus Christ from a field of barley. Even more astounding is that the man, Boaz, sees her in this busy field! Incredible! "Who is that girl?" he asks the help.

In the field. So let's talk a bit about the field. Over in the Book of Matthew, chapter 13, verse 38, Jesus explains the word "field." He says, "The field is the world." For our purposes here, we will relate the field to the world's system. Ruth's in the field. Men are in the field. Women are in the field. Ruth is gleaning behind the reapers. She's not in charge of anything. She owns basically nothing. She's a poor little Moabitess girl in a strange city, gleaning behind the reapers in a field of barley.

Over in the Book of Zechariah 4:10, the Bible declares, "Don't despise the day of small beginnings." New Testament scripture also tells us in the Book of Mark 10:31, "The first shall be last, and the last shall be first."

When Boaz inquired about Ruth, a servant explained who Ruth was, but her reputation had preceded her (Proverbs 22:1; Ruth 2:11-12). Everything and everybody were in that field but Boaz's eyes fell upon and were fixed on Ruth. Ruth's working. Ruth is gleaning behind the reapers. Ruth had a job, ladies! She wasn't just sitting on her hands, whiling the hours away. So we're in the field. Lots of men are there. What kinds of men are in the field?

In verse 2 of chapter 2 of Ruth, Boaz implores Ruth not to go to "other fields" and to "abide by my maidens." Um-m-m. Don't go all helter-skelter-nilly-willy to "other fields." Stick by people I know (Boaz said). Do what they do. Don't go elsewhere. Drink water here, because I know these people. Drink here when you're thirsty. (You can't drink everywhere, adies!)

Boaz tells Ruth, "I've advised the young men to stay away from you." Interesting dialogue, huh? Why would Boaz tell the young men to stay away from Ruth? Perhaps because he was well aware of their habits and proclivities, their character. He knew in some fields, predatory men hunted unsuspecting women.

In the field, if two animals are unequally yoked, they push and pull and cause abrasion to one another. In 2 Corinthians 6:14, the Bible tells us when one is born again, don't hook up with an unbeliever. Don't have mismatched dalliances (I call it "unholy alliances") with these kinds of men. The Bible tells us these relationships are "inconsistent" (Amplified Bible) "with our faith." It further says, "For what partnership does your right understanding; your right living, have with darkness or lawlessness?" (II Corin. 6:14).

"But", you say, "Lawless men are exciting." (Remember Bonnie and Clyde?) Wild men and wild women bring wild sex to the table, but usually, that's all they bring. Beware! Nothing spells Bozo like men who are highly skilled in the area of sexual pleasure. These men can be seducers. Men who may be totally unskilled elsewhere but rock your world in bed...

Guard your hearts, ladies, from strange affection. "Keep your heart with all diligence, for out of it flow the issues of life" (Proverbs 4:23). Develop a constancy of heart, purpose and honesty. "Develop steadfastness and a right goal in your Christian walk." Be alert in the field!

For you modern-day Ruths, the fields are vast, varied, and now virtual playgrounds, thanks to the internet. Use wisdom. The Bible says, "for she (Wisdom) is a teacher" (Proverbs 31:26; Proverbs 4). She calls to you every day, but are you listening? Listen to her as Ruth listened to Naomi's advice. Listen to her as Ruth listened to Boaz's advice about the fields of this life. It is when you listen that you will be supremely blessed.

Proverbs 4:8-9 tells us, "If you embrace wisdom fully, holding it in high esteem, you will be honored and blessed, and its presence will become an ornament of grace, a crown of glory."

Use wisdom in the fields of your relationships, ladies. Let it guide and teach you. Wear it as adornment and never let it go!

CHAPTER 6
-THE CHARACTER OF BOAZ-

"And Naomi had a kinsman of her husband, a mighty man of wealth, of the family of Elimelech, and his name was Boaz" (Ruth 2:1).

Boaz's wealth is usually emphasized when teaching from the Book of Ruth. Yes, Boaz was wealthy, but Ruth 2:1 tells us also that Boaz was a mighty man, conveying the idea of having qualities of the highest order, a gentleman. Apparently, Boaz was also highly esteemed in the community as well. Boaz was a straight-up m-a-n! Add to all of this, he was a kinsman redeemer.

Here in scripture, upon meeting Ruth, Boaz takes time to speak openly and honestly in the field to Ruth. He admonishes her to be aware while in the field, stay where it was safe, drink only from the vessels his people provided.

He's viewed as compassionate, thoughtful, caring, generous and attentive. Interestingly, he warned the young men to stay away from Ruth! He wanted to protect Ruth, thus he was seen as a protector.

In the Book of Ruth 2:11-12, Boaz lauded Ruth with praise. He'd heard about her kindness and her willingness to leave Moab to be with her mother-in-law Naomi, leaving her own family. Boaz seems to be very impressed with Ruth, indeed! From my spiritual antennae, Boaz deemed her a virtuous woman, and he wanted her to know just how impressed he was with her. (And don't we women, just like men, love praise?) "Why," Ruth asked, "have I found grace in thine eyes?" It seems Ruth was as impressed with Boaz as Boaz was with her. Self-effacing and humble, she graciously received Boaz's words.

Astoundingly, they found each other in the field and came together while she's working in his field! (Wouldn't you have loved to be there, seeing this meeting, hearing this dialogue?)

Provider. Protector. Boaz is seen also as a priest—a kinsman redeemer, a type of Christ, a man of character and standing. This was, and is, Boaz.

Perhaps Boaz noticed Ruth's style of dress, her mannerisms, how she moved. He knew she wasn't the usual women he would see working in the field. She stood out in that field!

He asks in Ruth 2:5, "Whose damsel is this?" One servant calls her a Moabitess, which rings like a slight. He tells Boaz she's a foreigner who had come up with Naomi. I believe that even from a distance, Boaz saw a difference–something, or rather, someone, refreshing and lovely.

Ruth found a Boaz she could believe in, in that field, on that day. My! My! You don't know where he is, ladies, but God does.

The Bible declares in the Book of Proverbs, "A good name is rather to be had than great riches..." (Proverbs 22:1). An intangible asset. A good name. A good reputation. Good character.

Check who you're dating. Ask around. Shake that apple tree!

The American Heritage Dictionary says "character" is the combination of qualities or features that distinguishes one person, group or thing, from another. Boaz stood out in that field and he stood up for Ruth. He was congenial, kind and interested in her. (How many men have you dated who only wanted to talk about themselves?) Bozos!

Boaz showed a real interest in Ruth. I can see him looking into her eyes as she spoke. He knew who he was! He wanted to know more <u>about her</u>. He was wealthy, but he was also highly esteemed in town. He possessed a good name and a good reputation. People revered him. His name was good.

Please look beyond what you hear, beyond the physical. It may be cliché', but "all that glitters isn't gold." You can just about hear Boaz's kind words, his advice to Ruth (Book of Ruth 2:8-14). She was, very possibly, intrigued by him.

What happens is as old as Father Time. We see who the man Bozo really is, but we close both our eyes and ears to what's as plain as the noses on our faces! When the stuff hits the fan, our friends restrain themselves from saying I told you so! Perhaps we'd been warned over and over and over, but we knew things would change, given time. But sadly, time and love prove futile. He is who he is: an arrogant, bombastic, belligerent, bellicose Bozo!

Remember: Character does count!

CHAPTER 7
-RUTH'S REP-

"And Boaz answered and said unto her, it hath fully been shown to me all that thou hast done unto thy mother-in-law since the death of thine husband..." (Ruth 2:11).

Boaz had already heard of Ruth. What had he heard? What is said about *you*? What have people heard? Does it ring true? Are you a woman revered?

According to the Book of Ruth, chapter 2, verses 11-12, Ruth asks Boaz, "Why have I found favor in your eyes that you should notice me, a foreigner?" The news of Ruth had been reported to Boaz fully. That is, someone had relayed the news that Ruth had been utterly kind to Naomi, her mother-in-law, since Ruth's and Naomi's husbands had died. A servant further tells Boaz that Ruth had left her homeland and her family to go to Bethlehem with Naomi.

It is then that Boaz generously pronounces a <u>blessing</u> upon Ruth: "The Lord repay your work and a full reward be given to you by the LORD GOD of Israel." (Ruth 2:12 Wow! What a man!

Boaz was attracted to Ruth's loyalty towards Naomi. Perhaps he found it quite remarkable, quite appealing. So do I. Such remarkable loyalty should be rewarded, thus Boaz pronounces (as a type of Christ) a blessing upon Ruth. He pronounces a reward over her right then and there! The loyal love Ruth displayed for Naomi surely moved Boaz. Boaz says it had been, "<u>fully</u> (Ruth 2:11) shown to him concerning Ruth's faithfulness to her mother-in-law, Naomi." You see, leaving one's homeland was a great sacrifice of loyal love.

When Boaz pronounced a blessing over Ruth for her loyal love and steadfast kindness and faithfulness towards Naomi, Ruth had found refuge in Boaz and in the God of Israel. I can just imagine that Ruth's heart was soaring at that point! (Wouldn't yours?)

A good reputation is of great magnitude, of great value. Proverbs 31:10 translates literally as "a noble wife." The scripture focuses on a woman's high status. Verse 26 tells us this woman possesses wisdom, kindness and nobility—great virtues. She's no sluggard! To add cream to the coffee, this woman fears the Lord! Remember: Ruth accepted Naomi's God in chapter 1, verse 16: "...your God shall be my God."

CHAPTER 8
-BOZOS - WHAT'S THEIR CHARACTER?-

"For men shall be lovers of their own selves...covetous, boastful, proud, unthankful, without natural affection...traitors, heady, high-minded...from such turn away..." (2 Timothy 3:1-7).

I've met quite a few men in my lifetime. Some with good character, and some not so much. Some moral. Some completely immoral!

Chilion and Mahlon, Ruth and Orpah's husbands in the Book of Ruth, had interesting names. Chilion's name meant sickly and weakly, while Mahlon's name meant weak and failing. Names are very important and they carry deep meaning and can allude to one's character. They may speak vociferously about who a person is. When he/she really is can be revealed by a person's name.

Weak men, sickly, failing men. Who is your man? What is his character? Men can be sickly and weak in their character. How? I want to use something here I heard on a Dr. Phil show one day. Dr. Phil used the term Evil Eight. He said women should watch out for this:

A person with a sense of entitlement

A person who has no remorse

An irresponsible person

A person who thrives on drama

A person who brags about outsmarting people

A person who has had many short-term relationships

A person who lives a life a fantasy

The well-known Dr. also referenced men he called BAITERS.

B - ackstabbers

A - rrogant

I - mposters

T - akers

E - gotistical

R - eckless

S - educers

Let's park here at seducers. It occurred to me one day that the serpent in Genesis chapter 2 was a bit of a seducer. "Hath God (really) said you should not eat from this tree?" he slyly asked Eve. I can imagine the entire conversation wherein the serpent spoke so very smoothly, almost seductively to Eve. Her mind went reeling! This crafty, wily creature talked Eve into tasting forbidden fruit from a tree—the tree of the Knowledge of Good and Evil, a tree from which God specifically told Adam and Eve not to eat! She began to doubt while conversing with the serpent. She ate the fruit, the Bible tells us, and gave some to her husband, Adam. (Evil desire is always attractive, isn't it?) Seducers are sly, wily, crafty, smooth pursuers of women who are vulnerable.

2 Timothy 3:5-6 TELLS US: "Avoid persons who <u>seem</u> <u>to</u> <u>have</u> a form of godliness... have nothing to do with them. They worm their way into homes of silly women and <u>gain</u> <u>control over</u> <u>them</u>..." Ladies, these men love themselves much more than they will ever love you. When you entertain such men, you leave the door wide open for all kinds of lustful desires. Avoid men who only want control over you. Men who want to bring you down.

Beware! Liars lie. Thieves steal. Seducers seduce. Some things are as clear as crystal. Stop thinking when you see a pattern of behavior that <u>you</u> can fix him. People who have negative patterns of behavior are not very attractive on the inside. What you must do is have the courage to see it for what it really is and have the courage to confront it. Look for genuine remorse for negative behavior. See if after the confrontation on his wayward behavior there is a willingness to change the behavior. Determine if the change is ongoing, or if that person only wants you to buy what they ae selling. Honesty is the hallmark of a relationship. Trust is key. Where there is no trust, there is no <u>relationship</u>.

Watch liars! People will lie, and they lie for various reasons. Some lie to protect themselves. Others lie to gain the upper hand. Still others lie to seem important. This is an apodictic list, I'm sure. Be reminded: The truth will win out! Ask yourself: Do I want a pathological liar for a husband? Marriage, after all, <u>is </u>forever!

Also, the Book of Genesis shows us <u>who</u> Satan really is: liar, thief, destroyer. (Genesis 3:1) The serpent was testing Eve's resolve. I'm sure she thought she had it all together in the garden. Then, along comes an ol' wily, crafty, clever serpent, a silver-tongue devil. With the voice of a true seducer, he beguiles Eve, seducing her one sentence at a time. His lips virtually dripping with lies wrapped up in sugar.

In the Garden of Delight, the serpent represents Satan's deceitful ways, his artful ability to steal, to destroy and to seduce or tempt. Don't ever believe you're not impervious to his tricks and schemes. You shouldn't "dance" with the devil!

Watch to see if your man seems to enjoy hurting you time and time again. Empathy is an important attribute; yet, he seems to lack it, showing little to no remorse when he hurts you. Ding! Ding! Ding!

His lies haunt you. He lies about his finances. He lies about his profession – about his marital status and/or sexual history. And, the list goes on and on, so be alert, ladies.

I vividly remember a young friend of mine who got engaged to a young man, seemingly of good character. At his invitation, she went home with him. Wherever she went, she got an earful of questionable reports. But she eventually got a beautiful ring! What to do! She asked me what she should do. My advice was "pray and weigh."

Take responsibility, ladies. You know in your spiritual heart this man is a Bozo, yet you keep changing the narrative about him—excusing bad behavior, not paying attention to every clue you get. You see yourself attracting this kind of man over and over! These guys are all about themselves and not about you! They're into themselves and not into you.

Don't go another day, another week, another year down this perilous path. These relationships are anemic, meaningless, meandering mishaps. You can and must require more of these men and more for yourself!

CHAPTER 9
BAITERS
-BRAGGING RIGHTS OR WRONGS-

"Pride goeth before destruction and a haughty spirit before the fall" (Proverbs 16:18).

Have you ever been in the company of a braggart? One who monopolizes an entire conversation with a symphony of I-I-I? "He's always on his mind." Initially, because he seems so appealing, your interest in him is very high, but as time goes on, you find you can't get a paragraph in about your day, or what's of interest to you. These are ego-trippers or possible narcissists.

The Bible talks about pride. Pride is dangerous. Pride is also very subtle. The Book of Proverbs 27:2 says, "let another praise thee, and not thine own mouth; a stranger, and not thine own lips. Braggarts are boring! Boorish! Bozos!

Pride may mask itself or present itself as confidence. You'll know the difference. The Bible tells us the fear of the Lord is to hate evil: pride and arrogancy. Pride can be ever so subtle. When it comes, the Bible says, "shame comes along with it."

In the Old Testament (Book of Daniel 4:33) Nebuchadnezzar's heart was filled with pride. God pronounced judgement in verse 32. This prideful king ended up grazing in the field, his hair grown out like feathers, and nails like eagle's talons. The Lord is serious about pride! It was only when this king recognized God's power, and gave Him praise, that the king was restored.

Baiters have the ability to lure you. They literally "set out bait." They sat traps for women. Baiters flatter and are often overly attentive. They hang out at supermarkets and at department stores, and yes, even at church.

Walk down any aisle at any grocery store, and you may see a baiter. He may have a cute, little child with him. When you comment on how cute the child is, the baiter flashes a toothy grin. At this point, the conversation starts, and he thinks, Ahh, I got her.

I'm not saying this is what is true for all "mankind," but if you're attracting jerks or Bozos, check yourself! There is a reason your antennae are set on channel B–O–Z–O. Perhaps you should start writing a journal, keeping track of some of his faux pas. This is not written to make you feel that you're so perfect but remember, you're looking for a life-long partnership, a marriage, not a messy mishap. Is this the person you want for the rest of your life? Forever is forever, ladies!

Reckless Men

Reckless men are exciting men. These men jump off cliffs. They hang glide. They drive fast, fancy cars. They take risks. Heedless men. Head strong. Rash men. Men who have "no regard," the American Heritage Dictionary says, "for consequences." Men like these are good in the moment, good for partying with, but not good for the long haul called marriage. And they need constant and new challenges. So ladies, tomorrow you may be old news as he seeks someone more thrilling. You may be yesterday's newspaper wrapping dead fish.

Please consider: What if this recklessness continues after the I do's? Are you prepared to put up with total disrespect? What if this recklessness includes him not wanting a monogamous relationship? Are you prepared to stay and to put up with such behavior?

Recklessness appearing under the guise of "exciting" may have you going too far too fast. Slow down and really assess what's going on and determine what you really want long-term. If this is all you want, then Hey!

So, what am I saying with all these types of men? Very succinctly, I want you to be prepared and comfortable with loneliness. While loneliness can be a sad, empty feeling, it is necessary as a teacher. You may feel incomplete, but you're not alone. The Lord is with you always! You learn in your loneliness to depend on God.

Stop staying in relationships that are well past their expiration dates. Milk curdles after expiration dates and it tastes really bad. It sours and is no good. You know in your inner man that the relationship is over. You know this relationship is destructive, even toxic, but you've shown such desperation. You should've kicked that zero to the curb, but you haven't. Why? Because you don't want to be alone. Alone is not alone, but rather it's an opportunity to develop you, to get to know yourself. Who are you really? What do you want? How can you reach and achieve your goals?

With your willingness to settle for less than God's best, you've limited God, tied His hands. Remember: If you want things your way, He'll let you have that Bozo! You get what you allow!

If you're involved with a loser right now, let him go today. Make up your mind that you're on a new track. Run your race and "press towards the mark for the prize of the high calling in Christ Jesus" (Phill. 3:14-15). Press your way! You'll get to where the Lord wants you to be. I promise you that! You'll get there by faith, unfeigned faith, and with the help of Almighty God.

My prayer for you today: May God guide you on your way.

CHAPTER 10
-FINDING A WAY TO FORGIVE-

"For if you forgive men their trespasses your heavenly Father will also forgive you: but, if you forgive not men their trespasses, neither will your heavenly Father forgive you your trespasses" (Matthew 6:1).

Some years ago, I was planning to do a teaching from New Testament Scripture on the subject of forgiveness. I won't soon forget the day I was watching PBS. I was about to change channels, when I distinctly heard the Lord say, "leave it." I knew that the Lord wanted me to see something important, something I needed to hear. Indeed there was! The day was fast approaching for the teaching, and I felt this program had something to do with it. I must share with you that prior to seeing the PBS program, I had read an article in Essence magazine about an

African girl from Rwanda who'd witnessed family, neighbors, and friends die by being macheted or hacked to death.

The article told of how a Good Samaritan (I believe he was a pastor) hid her and others behind a special partition in his home to save their lives. It was simply a fascinating and beautiful story about forgiveness. This was the kind of forgiveness most of us cannot fathom, lest known give.

As I watched the PBS special, I learned that as the Rwandan girl's family had been being massacred in a 1994 Rwandan genocide, she realized that forgiveness was her only option.

With civil war raging, the girl, Immaculee Ilibagiza, made a conscious decision to forgive genocidal attacks perpetrated against her people where nearly one million people were killed savagely by Hutu militants.

Immaculee and seven others were hidden in a pastor's bathroom where a wardrobe had been pushed in front of it. The Hutu militants came to the pastor's house and searched routinely. Immaculee and the others could hear the militants' conversation. Imagine their hearts beating wildly during these times! Imagine the fear of being found.

This was a PBS program the Lord really wanted me to see. As the man emceed the program and was about to introduce Immaculee, I formed a picture of her in my mind—tall, chocolate, silky skin, beautiful face, and articulate.

A choice to forgive when you know you should can be a heavy burden to bear, or not—it depends on your spiritual maturity and your willingness to do so.

When Immaculee walked out onto this big stage, I experienced sheer elation! I watched and attentively listened to this tall, willowy, beautiful black-complexioned young woman from thousands of miles away. Yet, I mused how universal forgiveness is, how close.

Immaculee spoke very eloquently and articulately about horrible atrocities no human should ever have to speak about, let alone witness.

Forgiveness. The Bible makes clear that forgiveness is not a *do you want to do it or not* thing, but rather, it is a commandment from Almighty God. One might say in one's naiveté, I just can't forgive. I say you can't afford not to.

Immaculee stated that while in the pastor's bathroom, she read from a Bible. The words from Luke 23:34 resounded in her ears: "Father, forgive them, for they know not what they do." As she read, forgiveness flooded her heart. She recounted: "I just simply wanted to feel better."

She wanted to <u>feel</u> <u>better</u>. Bitterness makes one feel bad. It affects you spiritually, physically, mentally and emotionally. It creates an acidic and toxic environment—a cesspool of woulda, coulda, shouldas and resentment.

Set Immaculee's situation aside for a moment. Let's talk about you. Why can't you forgive? If you're honest with yourself, you may realize that to some degree, you were duplicitous in your own situation. You were an enabler in situations that turned out badly. You may have helped derail that train that became a train wreck by compromising: "I believe he's not the best thing I've had, but I can work with that," or, "I realize this relationship's moving much too fast, but I don't want him to get away." What is he, a trout? Or, "I hear he's good at the game, but, I'm better at it than he is." Wrong on so many levels.

Let's go back for a minute to the Book of Ruth. In chapter 1, Naomi and Ruth are walking through a street in Bethlehem. Women are watching them as they walk, wondering if Naomi is <u>the</u> Naomi they remember: "Naomi, is that you?" they call out. It is then that Naomi replies: "Don't call me Naomi. Call me Marah, for the Lord has dealt very bitterly with me." Naomi "labels" herself "bitter" Marah. The many losses she's suffered have obviously changed her. Her name, Naomi, means "pleasant." Naomi's past experiences in Moab have caused her such grief. Through so much loss, she no longer carried the name Naomi or "pleasant." She was a broken and bitter woman. (I have wondered if Naomi needed to forgive someone.)

In any case, be very careful that you don't become bitter, that you don't become <u>what</u> <u>happened</u> to you. You are not what you've been through! You've been in the fiery furnace, but not even the smell of smoke is on you. You survived the flames of a lover's infidelity. You came through the heat and the horror of dishonesty. You learned that you can leap over the licking flames of lighter fluid-fueled liars and leeches.

Listen, God got Daniel out. He can do the same for you!

Some relationships end with visceral, viperous, and vitriolic attacks against the perceived offender. Some partners take to Twitter, Facebook, etc., to launch what I call ICBM's: intercontinental belittling bombs and missile-like rants about each other. It all fuels the fires of unforgiveness, making break-ups even worse.

You may be susceptible to hurling vituperative and venomous accusations on Facebook, but be careful, please. Acrimonious treatment of a former lover/partner will not satisfy you long-term. This behavior will not solve anything! Yes, the hurts are real, and while I sympathize and empathize with you, I don't agree with unforgiveness. You must forgive.

Yes, you feel betrayed. Yes, you're bitter. Perhaps like Naomi, you carry those scars inside and out. (I actually believe her bitterness changed her countenance!) You may even feel rage and perhaps you're entitled to it.

You say: "I just can't forgive this person or those persons." I'm here to tell you, you not only can, you simply must—to be blessed.

Immaculee was in a bathroom of unforgiveness, but her desire to get out, to be free, not only from the marauding militants, but also from the feeling of rage and bitterness that held her captive, drove her to the cross.

Don't allow unforgiveness into your heart. It has a way of growing what I call sucker roots. These roots spread out and grow deeper into your spiritual heart, causing you to stumble into bitterness as Naomi did. Perhaps she was so angry because her losses seemed so insurmountable and they simply overwhelmed her.

Is this a part of your unwillingness to forgive? Look at it another way: When you forgive fully, you're making room for the blessing that God Himself ordained for you from before the foundation of the world.

CHAPTER 11
-FORGIVING MEANS FORGIVING YOURSELF, TOO-

"There is therefore now no condemnation to them which are in Christ Jesus..." (Romans 8:1).

I fully understand why forgiveness means forgiving oneself, too. How very many of us have serious issues with forgiving ourselves? Something resides in us that says if we carry the cross of unforgiveness regarding ourselves, we're doing pious penance, and that is somehow a good thing. Wrong!

You are worthy of forgiveness even for yourself. Christ died for us all. The debt is paid in full with His precious blood. The Bible declares, "Now unto him who is in Christ Jesus, there is no condemnation" (Romans 8:1). None! At the cross! At the cross! That is where our forgiveness is. Sin was slayed there. Jesus conquered sin there once and for all.

The word "therefore" indicates a transition. Something happened. Jesus carried our sins to Calvary's cross and he nailed them to it.

Romans 8:1 goes back to the previous verse, Romans 7:25. We were, according to the Apostle Paul, wretches undone. Sin lived in our members. That's where the contest is. "Who," Romans 7:24 says, "will deliver me from the body of death?" Sin living in our members brings about spiritual death. So we need "back-up," outside help. This help only comes from the Lord. Evil/sin is in opposition to that which is good.

The Apostle Paul here in Romans stresses that there is only one who can deliver him (us). His Name is Jesus Christ! Paul realizes it, too, as stated in

Romans 7:18 states, "The flesh - sinful flesh - has no good thing residing in it. (The Spirit is willing, but the flesh is weak.)" Our deliverance comes through Christ Jesus. Praise God!

Christ stood in our stead. He alone hung on Calvary's cross to deliver us, to free us from the grip and the grasp of sin.

None of us can really appreciate our deliverance/victory until we understand the nature of the opposition.

Bottom line: Nothing we've done is so heinous, so horrible that when we're in Christ, His forgiveness won't cover it fully, firmly and forever! Glory to God! Look at how the Lord cares for and loves us!

I want you to notice also that in the Book of Luke, chapter 23, Jesus prayed for those who took His life! Talk about forgiveness! He prayed for those who flogged Him all night long. For those who cussed Him. For those who spat upon Him. For those who parted his raiment. Again, that's forgiveness!

On the cross at Golgotha's Hill, one thief accepts that Jesus is the Christ, while the other one scoffs and belittles him. Yet, through it all, He forgave all for all. "Father, forgive them," Jesus implores the Father, "for they know not _what_ they do." I want to park here for a few minutes to tell you a personal story. I won't go too deep, because I've chosen not to...

A couple of years ago, I was watching Christian television and Pastor Creflo Dollar was preaching. I'd decided I would change the channel, but just as suddenly, I decided to stay tuned. I recall Pastor Dollar saying, "Church, I had a few issues and I was beating myself up about it, when the Holy Ghost told me, "son, you did that out of fear." This part of the program was quite interesting to me, because as I'd been ready to change the channel, I'd been thinking about something that I went through years and years ago. When Dr. Dollar said the Holy Ghost told him he'd done some things out of fear, the Lord spoke to me and said, "that's what happened to you, daughter." You acted out of fear. The Holy Ghost told me further that I should stop beating myself up over this thing. God said He'd forgiven me a long time ago!

I must tell you, that day I was delivered! I realized I'd been reliving, rehearsing, and rehashing the event sub-consciously for years.

The Lord told me to let it go! And, so, Beloved, I share this with you and I implore you, too: Let it go! Today and forever. For the Bible declares, "we've all sinned and come short of the glory of God" (Romans 3:13). Ask God to help you get to a place of forgiveness for yourself. He will!

You, too, must and will come to epiphanies that will change your lives for the better. The Lord told me "let it go!" And, so Beloved, I implore you to "let it go!" Today and forever. Ask the Lord to help you get to a place of forgiving yourself.

I realized the day the Lord told me to release the thing to Him. It was tied to my mother and her opinion of me. Because my upbringing was fairly tumultuous (dare I say, strange), I was full of fear of my mother. Watching Dr. Dollar that day was a pivotal moment in my life.

We must remember one thief on Calvary's cross (Luke 23) received forgiveness, and he must have, at the very last, found eternal peace. One thief left the earth in a state of bitterness and unrest and unrepentance, even anger. The repentant criminal found forgiveness at the cross and ultimately he gained paradise. We gain absolutely nothing from unforgiveness!

Carrying unforgiveness against others, as well as ourselves, is a heavy, harmful, and burdensome weight to bear. Bear it no more, for the Bible declares in 1 John 1:9, "If we confess our sins, He (God) is faithful and just to forgive us for our sins and cleanse us from all unrighteousness." The word "confess" here means "agree with the Lord" about your sins, i.e., "say the same thing." Once you confess the sin(s), you forsake the sins(s). Confess to God, then God, who is faithful and righteous at all times, will forgive us and clean us up. Only He can do that! He gives us absolution from the penalty and pollution of sin. God is truly good. He doesn't want us <u>tortured</u> by the pitiful pasts we've all had.

So, this is your season to confess and let God have that heavy weight. You'll be surprised how when that weight is lifted, you'll not only feel better, but you'll look better. You will sleep better. You may even begin to hear people comment about "how good you look."

All of us have frailties, faults and have fallen. Everyone has slipped up, messed up, screwed up, and will continue to struggle in these areas, but we have an Advocate, Jesus Christ, the Righteous. Hallelujah! The Bible declares in Romans 3:23 "For <u>all</u> have sinned and come short of God's glory. The key here is to simply confess and allow God to do the rest. Bear in mind that what doesn't kill you makes you stronger.

It happened! It's over! You get on with your confession, and then live your life. God has promised abundant life--life to the fullest. A great life with your past sins in the rearview mirror.

It's your season. You've planted and you've watered (sometimes with your own tears). You are forgiven, so now believe to see the goodness of the Lord in the land of the living. From this moment on, live your life expecting to reap a great and glorious harvest from the Lord!

Yes, like the rest of us, you've made many mistakes. You've had some bumpy roads. I'm the first to admit, there have been so many things if I could do them over, I would do them differently.

I finally and thankfully realized that God will forgive almost anything when we ask Him to. I say "almost anything" because He says plainly that there are some things He will not forgive. Suicide is one of them. (Exodus 20:13, Deut. 30:19, Job 1:21, I Corin. 6:19-20).

Ladies, we live in a society where people don't seem to know how to "pass through" adversity, hardship, difficulty, i.e., loss of a child, loss of a job, etc. You may feel as though you're lost in a densely populated forest where you can't see daylight. All you have is a small ax with which to chop your way to freedom. So you start chopping and soon you want to just give up.

Here's a story I've heard my pastor tell for years, and I'm paraphrasing: "A man was lost in the woods. He started to chop trees, and he chopped so fiercely, he grew tired and wanted to give up. He did not know that he was only three trees away from getting out of that forest! Three trees away from civilization!" I guess the moral of this story is don't give up!

Sometimes we see opposition—i.e. missteps, mistakes and mess-ups as just that—opposition. God sees opposition as an opportunity to grow.

The 23rd Psalm tells us, "yea, though I walk <u>through</u> the valley..." The operative word is <u>through</u>. You must keep on going. Go through; don't get stuck where you are. Stuck in the valleys of your life. Stuck in unforgiveness. Walk on through. Take that opposition and turn it into opportunity. Use those negative experiences to grow and to know. <u>Grow</u> in grace. Know that God has only planned good for you. Get ready for the good things God has prepared for you from before the foundation of the world. Forgive yourself. Let go and live your best life! It's just a few trees away. Chop! Chop! Chop!

CHAPTER 12
-GETTING WHAT YOU NEED-

"The Lord grant you that ye may find rest, each of you in the house of her husband..." (Ruth 1:9 KJV).

Rest. The Lord grant you rest in the house of your husband.

So, what is it that Naomi wanted for her daughters-in-laws? It's obvious that she loves and cares about these women. Naomi was thinking that perhaps at some point the girls would want to remarry. Just as the girls had been faithful during times of adversity, Naomi wanted God to give them blessing and prosperity now as perhaps they entertained second marriages.

Let's go deeper with the word rest because this word has weightier significance. Yes, rest denotes prosperity in marriage, but it also has implications for having children. The proper Hebrew word is "Manoah." Financial success. Children. A godly marriage with great benefits. Naomi wanted her girls to be well cared for. (Isn't that what all mothers want for their children?) Rest or "Manoah" is something you who are seeking marriage should want for yourselves. It is much desired. "The Lord grant you that ye may find rest…" I must add: Be very careful where and in whom you seek rest, where you seek comfort, blessing, and prosperity.

In Ruth chapter 1, Naomi admonished her daughters-in-law to <u>return</u> to their homeland. One did. One didn't. You should make an informed, godly decision about what you want and remain steadfast. Don't settle. You can't be in relationships when you're weak. You must go in from a position of strength. You must be whole, healthy, and of sound body, mind, and spirit. Otherwise you won't be able to contribute much to a relationship. Please know and understand that what you want may not be what you need. God Himself knows the difference. Realistically, sometimes we cannot distinguish the difference for ourselves.

Getting what you need requires knowing God's will for you. The song says, "What God has for me is for me." But, are you sure <u>this</u> relationship's for you? Does it come with so much drama that you're constantly traumatized? If that's true, re-evaluate, reassess, and maybe you'll have to relocate.

Again, pray, weigh, and may I add, <u>wait</u> (on the Lord).

CHAPTER 13
-SPECIFICITY-

"What do you want me to do for you?" (Mark 10:51).

The Lord listens to our heart's desires. He alone knows them. I believe that when one prays, he/she should pray specifically.

When you pray, don't go around the mulberry bush with God. He already knows that's going on with you, yet He tells us to "ask." He is not a Wizard of Oz-type God, far away in some mystical land. You don't have to jump through hoops or skip down the yellow brick road. God is a real Being. He is God! He's about relationship.

The Bible declares: "He knows our down-sitting and our uprising." It further declares, "He knew us before we were knit in our mother's womb" (Psalm 139).

So now I ask you: What do you want? What can God do for you?

I recall in my old strict Baptist Church, church deacons would lead the devotion. Words would come out in a flurry of flowery and seemingly foreign words. I was quite young and so I had no clue of what they were praying about. None! I've found out that the Lord isn't impressed with the multiplicity of words. He's more interested in the sincerity of our hearts.

I have experienced God stopping me from praying one way to praying another. I guess the words were either too many or too insincere. Who knows! But He led me by His Spirit.

In Mark 10:51; a man called Bartimaeus calls out to Jesus for help. His cries grow in intensity. He shouts louder as the crowd tries to shut him up, whereupon Jesus asks, "What do you want me to do for you?" What do you want Jesus to do for *you*? You must be real and real specific with the Lord.

I've heard so many women say, "I want a husband," or, "I want to be married". Listen, you can get a husband on any street corner, under any street lamp. Get real specific in prayer. Tell God what it is that you desire.

Personally, I know what it is like to have the Lord ask what I need of Him. It is mind-blowingly awesome! The Lord loves specificity.

In the text about blind Bartimaeus, Jesus' healing of this blind man was in response to Bartimaeus' faith. He recognized Jesus as Messiah, as Lord, as the One who could help him. What did Bartimaeus want? What was the deepest desire of his heart? To recover his sight!

Bartimaeus' faith caused him to recover his sight, to have it restored. (Some theologians feel he was not always blind.)

Bartimaeus was admonished to "be quiet!" I love the way he keeps on yelling until Jesus responds.

Matthew 7:7 admonishes us to "keep on asking, keep on seeking, and keep on knocking, that your deficiencies may be met from the Divine Supply." Pray frequently for all your needs. God pays close attention and looks with

close observation to our prayers. While Matthew 6:8 tells us that God knows what we have need of before we ask, He still tells us to ask! He also regards our motives in the asking, so be very careful that your heart's motivations are right. Unworthy motives are exercises in futility. Just be sincere and open with God, talking to Him as a good friend, because that is who He is!

Tell the Lord how you want to be married, have a life-long companion, have children and live a godly life. He cares about our cares and our deepest desires: "Casting all your cares upon Me; for I careth for you," i.e., what concerns us is of the utmost concern to Almighty God.

You need to be—you've got to be—specific with God.

S - p - e - c - i - f - i - c - i - t - y!

CHAPTER 14
-WHAT A WAY TO END!-

(Ruth 4:10)

Notice in chapter 4 of Ruth, the number 10 is used in verse 2. Ten was considered a quorum required for a synagogue. Ten was also required for the marriage benediction.

Verse 3 says Naomi had a parcel of land for sale. The idea here in scripture is to help this family to stay afloat so as not to suffer extinction. The family would be preserved. Providentially, the problems of the two women, Naomi and Ruth, were also the problems of the community.

In verse 4, there is a kinsman closer to the deceased Elimelech, so he is rightly informed. He gets "first dibs" at buying the land. He **only wanted** the land, so he thought that buying it only would seal the deal. But, he would have had to marry Ruth, have a son by her, and hold the land in trust for Ruth's son! This son would inherit the name and patrimony of Mahlon, Ruth's deceased husband. (The plot thickens!)

So, in chapter chapter, the kinsman decides (verse of 4), "I cannot redeem it!" Why? Because he would lose as a purchaser. This deal would hurt him, because the land would not belong to him, but to Ruth's son. This transaction was the law of the "goel," or the "Kinsman Redeemer."

In verse 8, the first kinsman tells Boaz: "Hey! You should buy it!" In verse 9, Boaz does just that! One shoe of Boaz's comes off to seal the deal, so that the deceased man's name "be not cut off."

Verse 11 shows some persons are heard offering blessings over Boaz and Ruth's home: "The Lord make the woman...like Rachel and like Leah

"Jacob's wives....and be famous in Bethlehem..." (Gen. 46:26; Ruth 4:11). The people here express a prayer that Boaz's family would be rewarded comparable to Jacob's family. The words "to be famous" were translated "call a name." This prayer called for the children's names to be reckoned descendants of Boaz.

Verse 13 shows Boaz taking Ruth as his wife, and she bore him a son, "a sacred trust from the Lord." Even Naomi's blessed, as the child that Ruth bore for Boaz was a "restorer of her life." Now her family line could continue. Hope for Israel!

Ruth bares Boaz a son named Obed. Obed means "worshiper" or "servant."

What a story! Ruth, our narrative's heroine, a Moabitess girl, marries a wealthy, highly esteemed, highly revered Brother Boaz of Bethlehem. Ruth's determination to have a new life and a new God, places her footprints down in the sands of Biblical history for all eternity. These footprints write her name indelibly in a very important Biblical narrative, sealing her lineage and her DNA in King David's family, and in the lineage of our Lord and Savior Jesus Christ.

Through loss and sorrow, through trials and tribulations, Ruth journeyed to find love and prosperity in Bethlehem. Her story is one that resounds with a hallelujah chorus of laudatory testimony to God's goodness, His love and providential care for His people. It shows how God can take the least of us and lift us up.

At a time when loyalty and righteousness were in short supply, enter Ruth, exhibiting faith unfeigned!

Who knows where your footprints will lead you! Who you will meet in your Bethlehem!

CHAPTER 15
-THE LAST WORD-

I want to close by saying it is good to act and make good choices based on information that is honest and <u>godly</u>. Conversely, "it is dangerous to have," the Bible says, "zeal without knowledge, and the one who acts hastily makes poor choices" (Proverbs 19:2).

We don't know for how long Naomi had been discussing her "move" back to Bethlehem. What we do know is that Ruth decided to go with her, and Orpah decided not to go.

Each day we face numerous choices: what to wear to work, what to eat for lunch, how to respond to difficulty, etc.

Certainly, in making these choices, one should utilize, as we discussed, wisdom, for she is a teacher.

Also, Proverbs 3:5-6 tells us, "Lean not to thine own understanding. In all thy ways acknowledge (God), and He will <u>direct</u> thy path."

In making your choices, Philippians 4:8 says: "Finally, my brethren, whatever is true, honorable, right, pure, lovely, of a good repute, dwell on these things."

When Ruth was faced with making the choice between Moab and Bethlehem, we can't say for sure how her decision-making process went. Did she ask Naomi a lot of questions? Were her emotions on edge? What kind of information did Ruth have?

One should do as my pastor, Apostle Julius H. Kidd, told us in a Bible study years ago: "Decide if it's <u>pressing</u>, or <u>pressing and urgent</u>?

I see women who, when choosing a mate, feel that if they don't decide quickly, the opportunity will pass. Others may allow friends or relatives to "make up their minds" for them.

One must delve deep, searching their own heart's motivations. The Bible says, "A dog will return to its own vomit" (Proverbs 26:11) Are you such a one? One prone to repeating bad habits? (Remember: Your six-foot-five may just be the five-foot-seven you dumped last week online!)

The same temperament! The same messy Marvin. So be very, very careful! You don't want to get stuck in Moab!

Always let wisdom guide you. You must have it to keep from falling down in the muck and miry clay of Moab. Don't miss warning signs we call "red flags." If someone sees something you don't see, listen! "In an abundance of counselors, you'll have the victory" (Proverbs 11:14). Remember: Don't be afraid to see what you see. Your time for avoidance has runout. Face truth fearlessly.

Let go of myths: "Well, I'm special. I can change him," or, "I just may be the exception to the rule."

Do the math. Assess potential risks. Don't think you have to be reckless and ruthless. Think: What is God doing for me in this season? Realize that when He moves, you should join Him.

My fervent prayer, Beloved, is that the Lord would prosper you. Your life is beginning from the first page of this book to the last page. Believe that the Lord has only promised you good, and the best is yet to come!

-<u>Pray the Prayer</u>-

As we got deeper into the Boaz ministry, the Holy Spirit gave me a prayer for the young women (and older) that I minister to. I call it the Boaz Prayer. In the Old Testament, we see the children of Israel in constant sin due to disobedience. Come with me to the Book of 1 Samuel, chapter 16. Here we see the Prophet Samuel is sent by the Lord to Jesse the Bethlemite's house to anoint the next king of Israel. Samuel takes his oil with the intent of doing just that. Here in scripture, we see Jesse's sons come out to the prophet. Each son is as handsome as the next. I want to point out something to you before we go any further, found in 1 Samuel 16, verses 7-8 (KJV):

Interestingly, when the first boy comes out, the Lord tells Samuel <u>not </u>to look on the height or the boy's stature—not to look at the boy's outer appearance. He tells Samuel this one He's <u>refused</u>. He says further, "For the Lord sees not as man sees, for man looks on the outer appearance, but the Lord looks on the heart." The Lord spoke these words in reference to Jesse's son, Eliab. Still more interesting in verse 8, the Lord says to Samuel these words concerning Jesse's son Abinadab: "Neither has the Lord chosen <u>this</u>." (Not him, but "<u>this</u>.")

Verse 9 is shockingly similar! In verse 10, Jesse's other sons passed before Samuel, and the Lord says to Samuel as Samuel relays the message to Jesse: "The Lord has not chosen these." (No ringing endorsements here!) I find the language here fairly strong, yet it's clear as crystal. The Lord had not chosen any of these!

The salient question is asked of Jesse by the prophet in verse 11: "Do you have any more sons?" It is then that Jesse's son David is sent for. Enter David, a young sheep herder. David is said to be "the one" by the Lord, so the prophet anoints him as King over all Israel. Although quite young, the Lord knew David's heart, so He knew who He wanted as King. (Similarly, He knows who He wants for you.)

Now, the ceremony of anointing David is quite curious, because at that time Israel had a King. Yes! Saul was already sitting on the throne! Saul is a very handsome man, ladies. The Bible declares, "he stood head and shoulders against the rest" (I Samuel 10:23). Yet, sadly, Saul had a few issues, among which was that he was a "taker." Remember, I quoted to you what the moniker "BAITERS" meant: The "T" stood for Taker. That's who Saul was. (Don't be afraid to see what you see!)

In verse 22 of 1 Samuel chapter 8, the prophet Samuel is told to give the people who they wanted. Also, God said for Samuel to tell the people what Saul would do <u>to them</u>, how much he would <u>take from</u> them.

Ladies, takers take, and taking can cause you heavy loss—sometimes irrevocable loss. The loss can be financial, physical, mental or emotional, or all of these.

Eliab, Abinadab and Jesse's other sons, didn't pass the smell test. Let's look at 1 Samuel chapter 17. Here a little more light is shed about Jesse's sons. Let's walk in the light. You know the story.

There's a battle being waged between the Israelites and the Philistines in the valley of Elah. Jesse, David's father, sends little David to the valley—sends a little sheep herder to the site of the battle to take food to his brothers. In verse 13, we see the three eldest sons of Jesse—Eliab, the firstborn, Abinadab, and Shammah on the battlefield. When David shows up with food, he is eyed suspiciously in verses 28-29. We see that there seems to be a little sibling rivalry between the brothers: "Why did you come down here, David? You just came to be nosey. You just want to show out!" One might surmise that this discourse is just a small part of what David was up against at home! Perhaps this is partly why these brothers were rejected by God to be anointed King over Israel.

Quoting Maya Angelou again: "When someone shows you who they are, believe 'em."

Whatever is in you will eventually come out of you. "Out of the heart flow the issues of life" (Proverbs 4:23). You job is to believe it when you see it. A Bozo is a Bozo!

These young men, David's brothers, were rejected by Almighty God! God Himself nixed them as king! My question to you is: If God rejects Bozos, why do you accept what God has rejected?

I have been so befuddled by story after story of unrequited love, or love on the skids, that I asked the Lord to help me help the women. Give me a prayer, Lord, I implored. Thus, the Boaz Prayer. It has been most helpful, and it works!

The Boaz Prayer is stated thusly, based on what the Holy Spirit gave me from 1 Samuel, chapters 8 and 16:

"Father God, in the Name of Jesus, if this man is not

My Boaz, remove him expeditiously, before I suffer loss.

It's in Jesus' name I do pray and give thanks. Amen!"

Simple! Succinct! Works!

I have had women pray the prayer and one of two things happened: either the boyfriend, lover, fiancé, or live-in got gone, or he put a ring on it. Also, I had a couple of women I'd admonished to pray the prayer, but the Holy Spirit told me, "they will not pray it, so you pray it for them." So, I did. Thankfully, the boyfriends (both of them), proposed and both couples got married, I'm happy to report.

Ladies, the prayer works! If nothing else, if the guy you're presently with leaves, he's only making room for a real Boaz, a real husband. The one the Lord has for you. Let me remark here this is no magic talisman. Truly God has the last say-so.

This prayer puts the ball squarely in God's court. When you place it in His hands, He moves. He intercedes/intervenes on your behalf.

The children of Israel in 1 Samuel 8 wanted a king like the nations around them. The Lord God had the prophet Samuel tell his people what this king would do to them. None of these "things" were good things. They were bad things, negative things, things that caused loss, suffering, i.e., forced labor, enumerated military service, and service in the royal arsenal, appropriation of their lands to reward the king, taxation, and confiscation of slaves for the king's service, etc. The Bible says the prophet Samuel "rehearsed" these matters to God's people, meaning he spoke them over and over and over! (How many times have you had relatives, family, and/or friends tell you "this dude" is all about taking, all about loss? But, you didn't listen.)

–**Summary**–

In the Book of Ruth, our heroine arrives in Bethlehem with her mother-in-law Naomi during barley harvest time. Ruth is the new girl in town, young and perhaps a bit anxious, a woman totally dependent on her mother-in-law. She had left her homeland. She'd left behind her pagan religion and her gods to start over in Bethlehem.

What a huge decision for a young widow to have to make, especially considering the magnitude of her losses.

Leaving Moab as a Moabitess woman, a worshiper of pagan gods, like her family before her, had to be a difficult thing for Ruth to do. Perhaps she felt at this point that her life was turned upside down. Who wouldn't! I can only imagine the trepidation she felt.

At barley harvest time, enter Naomi and Ruth (Orpah having turned back into Moab). Naomi and Ruth made their choices, and their commitment birthed love, loyalty and destiny. Destiny delivered purpose. Their relationship showed solidarity and steadfast devotion, one for the other. Ruth clung to Naomi as she chose Bethlehem and Israel's God. Ruth stuck with Naomi. She stuck by her.

Just as Ruth chose wisely and got out of Moab, so can you. You, too, can start again. You, too, can be free of the loss of the land called Moab. You, too, can have a new life. "He whom the Son sets free is free indeed" (Mark 10:45). Just let that marinate in your spirit for a moment. What a major and miraculous decision Ruth made! At every juncture, Naomi's admonition for Ruth to go back to her homeland (Moab) was met with the word, No! Ruth marries Boaz, a man of good character, a mighty man of valor and wealth.

Through this short but powerful Bible narrative we are shown what steadfast love and loyalty look like. In this Old Testament narrative, we clearly see a picture of Christ's love and His providential care for His own.

For her determined and courageous choice, Ruth now occupies a very important and celebrated place in Biblical history. She steps boldly into the lineage of our Lord and Savior Jesus Christ. She is His ancestress and an ancestress of King David, sweet Psalmist of Israel. She becomes a worshiper of Israel's God. Her faith exemplifies a belief in God and shows what God can do for His children's sake.

For her choice, Ruth was well rewarded.

Glory to God!

God speed to you on your own personal journey to Bethlehem.

Are you Saved? (Would you like to be?)

I cannot and will not assume that everyone who reads this book is saved. So I must ask you to give ear to salvation today, right now.

Salvation is the free gift of God, available to you right here, right now, today! Repeat this simple prayer and agree with me:

"Father God, I confess to you that I have sinned. But I ask You, Lord, to forgive me for all my sins. Cleanse me from all unrighteousness, and save my soul. I confess JESUS as my Lord and my Savior. I ask Him to come into my heart, save me, and fill me with the Holy Ghost. Baptize me in the name of Jesus. I thank you for saving me this day, and I commit to live for you from now on. In Jesus' name I pray and give thanks. Amen!"

I assure you that if you prayed that prayer, and meant it, today you are saved, born again, and are a new creature in Jesus Christ.

God bless you as you continue your spiritual journey!

ABOUT THE AUTHOR

Shirley A. Myers was born on the Mississippi Gulf Coast in a small city called Moss Point to the late Mr. J.P. Miller and Mrs. Emma Miller. She is the second oldest of eight children.

Educated in the segregated south, Shirley credits her teachers for instilling a profound love for writing.

After college, Mrs. Myers married her husband of 48 years, Gordon. They have four children. Eight years after marrying, the couple moved to Georgia, where Mrs. Myers has taught elementary school for 37 years. In 2001, Mrs. Myers was called to preach. In 2005, Mrs. Myers opened her home to start a women's Bible study, which she taught for four years. This became one of the most rewarding times of her life.

She has now combined her love of teaching and her love for the Word of God with the release of her first book, Do you Want a Bozo or a Boaz?

Mrs. Myers and her husband presently reside in the greater Atlanta area.

www.ingramcontent.com/pod-product-compliance
Lightning Source LLC
Chambersburg PA
CBHW060951040426

42445CB00011B/1106